SMARTERMARKETING *'Be a smarter marketer, be in control'*

**For CEOs everywhere… & aspiring ones!
the inside secrets on…
creating better customer relationships
to build bottom line profits**

SmarterMarketing
Formula for CEOs
(B2B version)

Contact details:

True Business Data Activation (TBDA Ltd),
(formerly The Business Development Agency),
Albury Hall, Albury,
Guildford, UK
GU5 9AD
Tel: +44 1483 20 20 55; Fax: +44 1483 20 36 37
www.tbda.co.uk; www.smartermarketing.co.uk
rick.pullan@tbda.co.uk
rick@thepullans.co.uk

Why this book?...

The majority of CEOs don't trust marketers' ability to deliver growth and the majority of Corporate Boards don't have Marketing Directors on them. So say several recent media reports. It doesn't matter which specific reports they are, the issue is that there is a worrying challenge to be addressed. Because when it's the custodian of customer connection, the Marketer, that's losing the vote of confidence, trouble is looming for business. This is why the time honoured SmarterMarketing formula is being published in book form.

Many business folk have graduated to the website (smartermarketing.co.uk) where, for a token fee, detailed 'how to' appendices provide implementation templates to complement the 'what to do' guidance given here.

It's lonely at the top for CEOs. You're constantly in the spotlight, with people waiting for you to trip up. Empowerment and values are crucial for quality teamwork to deliver goals. But how do you ring-fence the challenging debates and lengthy discussions in a straightforward, relaxed, informed and non-threatening way? And review delivery at suitable intervals? And train and coach whilst empowering and motivating and inspiring your team?

Formulae help. Tried and trusted formulae. Here's a 2 decade proven one for commerce. You might find it useful. If not I'll give you your money back. There's little risk anyway, just the cost of a book. Or even if you use the www.smartermarketing.co.uk website, it's just the price of a business lunch for 2, or the cost of a tankful of fuel for your executive car. There will be one thing at least you can learn and apply. The rest is a bonus. The power is the brevity and succinctness, because that's how you easily internalise the formula. No long videos or webinar programmes, just simple, succinct stuff you can use on a day to day basis to inspire, empower and manage the marketers working for you.

Enjoy, scare, build respect, eliminate bullshit, protect and build your bottom line using the business development blueprint exposed here.

SmarterMarketing Contents
Stages 1, 2 & 3

Page

Stage 2 – the 6 power steps to profitable success

In the manual toolbox, not this book...www.smartermarketing.co.uk

In the manual toolbox, not this book… www.smartermarketing.co.uk

Stage 3 – how to create & sustain a crm culture
(***the*** crm epiphany)

Introduction and market dynamics

Setting the mindset

C4 – the key 4 'customer' types

M4 – the 4 crucial 'management' tasks

R – containing 'relationship' issues

Introduction to SmarterMarketing
(what it is & why it's needed)

Learn Today's Critical Challenge For The World's Top Marketers

What is SmarterMarketing? It is a toolbox for fixing things in business, so that the key functions are aligned to creating customer profitability and stakeholder satisfaction.

The quest by companies for growth and scale is contagious. There has been an all-out drive for globalisation (versus community protection), increasing automation and super power control in the interests of economies of scale and a way of coping with the massive global correction since 2008.

The rate of change and pace of change is fast. Yet there is an inverse relationship between size or scale and the personal touch. With all this globalisation and automation, the individual customer can often feel unimportant or insignificant unless they're satisfied by the intrusions of social media involvement.

This is a compromise that professional marketers should fear, an issue that must be addressed.

It's a concern that is actually the responsibility of all senior management. Yet marketing has more impact (than other business activities) on developing competitive advantage and must drive the business agenda to deliver more corporate value. So a lot rests on marketers' shoulders. The finger of responsibility and accountability is pointing very much at the marketer's office. Some recent research collaboration between Professor Philip Kotler, PA Consulting Group, Marketing Forum Europe, Future Foundation Projects and Vox Pops International has identified some critical challenges...

...the marketers interviewed saw their main goal as developing brands for the long term, developing brand strategy and innovation and developing their people and capabilities. They see their most significant challenges as customer related - loyalty, innovation and insight. However, if marketers are to truly drive business success, they must make a major contribution to create long-term shareholder value. Yes, customer focus and creating customer value is important for the health of the business. But it's not enough. The long-term health depends on securing a stream of investment for marketing and development activities. This means meeting shareholder and investor expectations, by explaining (and being prepared to change) the marketing agenda in relation to the business direction, and reviewing performance against targets.

This in turn means marketers must align their goals and targets with profitability, not just top line sales growth. Therefore marketers must increase their skills in financial analysis, profit accountability and attribution, and improve their relationships with and interactions with the other major business functions.

In summary, marketing effectiveness must focus on the top line (sales, market share) **and** the bottom line (profits). *The research results showed that companies in which marketers have addressed these issues deliver an extra 2.6% total shareholder return, an incremental £26,000 per £1 million. Furthermore, companies whose CEOs have marketing experience generate 5.3% greater 'total shareholder value' than those that don't, an incremental £53,000 per £1 million of value. And finally, those companies that managed their investors well generated 6% more total shareholder value, a whopping extra £60,000 per £1 million value.*

Your 3 Stages To Success

Use SmarterMarketing - it will help you develop your business. It will show you how to think 'smarter' about marketing and business development. There are 3 Stages to master for clever marketing that will increase your product's market share or deliver the business growth you are seeking.

Stage 1 has to be mastered before moving to Stage 2. Similarly Stages 1 & 2 need to be understood before moving to Stage 3. In this book we cover Stages 1 & 2.

Our promise is to give you techniques that will create net extra sales and brand growth. Proven over time, it's worked for many famous brand names like Office Depot & Viking Direct (office products), Roomservice by Cort (office refurbishement), Costco, Polycom (telecoms) Toshiba, Europcar (car rental), Fujitsu (computers / IT), Panasonic (consumer durables), Caterpillar (trucks), Marks & Spencer (foods / retail), AJ Products (warehouse and office furniture). It's worked for many charity and service organisations in both the private and public sectors. It's worked for many smaller niche products too.

Benefits 2U

How will this SmarterMarketing book benefit C-suite? It's for people who do marketing, or want to do marketing, or have marketing people reporting to them.

If you're a small company or organisation:

- It is a proven source of rapidly understanding how to implement priority marketing activities that will strengthen revenue streams
- It offers massive time and cost saving versus outsourcing to marketing agencies.

If you're a medium to large company or organisation:

- It provides guidance in the form of an empowerment framework and terms of reference, to prioritise activities for employees, management and directors in an ever-changing personnel or trading environment. It is a management tool for directors and CEOs and a learning tool for today's marketers.

For your junior marketers:

- Quite simply, it is 'fast-track' learning for quicker 'on the job' effectiveness, enabling you to leapfrog several stages of apprenticeship and get recognised quickly.

For the CEO role this SmarterMarketing formula will help you work better with marketers and suppliers because you will have a mental checklist of crucial tasks that need to be implemented and an operating framework for managing activity implementation.

This book is short, and text intensive, for a very good reason. So you can fix the crucial operational parameters in your mind quickly and memorably, never to be forgotten. If it were a long treatise it would be just like many other business books or courses. Loads of good content (you know the sort of thing, 400 page manual, 2 or 3 days of seminar boot camp video), but how do you actually get your mind round it, how do you remember where to look for it, where is it filed? How can you refer to it if you're out of the office? How do you remember how to apply it day by day? Here, less is more. What you are paying for is the succinctness, the strategy agenda, the overview, the crucial formula into which any detail can be put into context, judged, prioritised and organised.

At this point it is important to govern your expectations. This is not about the technicalities of how to do good advertising, write good copy, embrace social media, do good PR, product design or NPD. These are technicalities you must learn elsewhere.

Take a step back - **this is about something more important, it's about people and it's about how to make live connections with those people that want it and that matter to your business.**

In essence, business is about people and their skills and how they conduct themselves. It's people (individuals in fact) that buy, or don't buy your product. It's people that design and make your product. It's people that sell your product and administrate your business. It's people that invest in your business.

By following the steps in this book, you will become better at influencing all these different types of peoples' attitudes and behaviour.

Before we go into detail, it's important that your thinking is set up properly - that your thinking is set up to respond to change, to predict change, to be prepared for it and manage it. Then all other activities will slot into place. Here it is...

...in commercial life, you can't do everything yourself. But you can understand everything that has to be done.

Governing or influencing the activities of all the different kinds of people that affect your business is what creates profit. But not just short term profit. Mastering the processes we cover in this book is the route to sustainable profit, profit year in year out, often referred to as 'quality profit'.

Learn The Secret Of CRM

In summary, the easiest way to comprehend CRM is to turn it on its head, or look at it backwards. What we mean by CRM is MRC - the management of relationships (and relevance) with customers - a marketing, intellectual business attitude issue, not an IT driven issue.

We are also assuming you already have a product and distribution system in place. Here we are talking about strengthening your relationships with customers, in essence the process of building **loyalty.**

This is not about the 4Ps of marketing, product, price, place, promotion. It's not about the 5 Ws, who, what, when, where, why...and then how. These are useful time-honoured checklists, but this is beyond that, because it's a blueprint of **practical implementation**, not just theory.

It's about a mindset, a discipline that takes the ambitious marketer into a different operational dimension, a different dimension of effectiveness and recognition, hopefully promotion and success.

This is a 'fast-track' program for achieving marketing communication effectiveness and accountability. The aim is to save you time, to focus your mind on the critical issues, to save you years of trial and error and learning by experience, to provide you with an ongoing professional working framework, agenda and checklist.

This book will show you how to create clever marketing activity that will increase your product's market share, build corporate revenue and profitability by maximising the profit of each customer/end user.

Spend your time on these crucial marketing activities, all else is secondary.

The principles apply in any market, any country and for any rank in any size of organisation.

Formulae Make Our World Go Round

Formulae are vital to comprehending our lives and evolution. They're often taken for granted and you might not be conscious of them on a day to day basis, but why are formulae so important and fundamental to our existence? The one that revolutionised astronomy, **$r3/T2 = constant$** (where r is the radius of orbit and T is time period for one cycle) was created by Johannes Kepler, 1571-1630, who was noted for the conception and verification of the 3 laws of planetary motion. So what, you could say. Well, these laws are known as Kepler's Laws, fundamental to the understanding of our solar system.

Yet another vital formula is **$F=Gm1m2/r2$**, where F is the force of mass 1 on mass 2, m1 is the mass of one object, m2 is the mass of another object, G is the gravitational constant and r is the distance between 2 objects. This formula was created by Sir Isaac Newton, 1642-1727, one of the greatest scientific intellects of all time. So what, you might say again; well the formula represents the definition of gravity, critical to our existence on planet earth, which we all just take for granted!

Remember **$e = mc2$**, in which energy is put equal to mass, multiplied by the square of the velocity of light. This showed that very small amounts of mass may be converted into a very large amount of energy and vice versa. The amazing discovery was that mass and energy were in fact equivalent, according to the formula, created by Albert Einstein, 1879-1955. A brilliant thinker and the best known scientist of the 20th century, his general theories of relativity and the particle nature of light changed the way we look at the world and revolutionised scientific thinking. The implications of the formula are still beyond our technological reach... just!

Unlock Your Business Potential

Formulae are vital to comprehending our lives and evolution. The SmarterMarketing formula is a wonderful self-auditing power tool - it enables you to see the way ahead from where you are now. The business formula for good marketing communications that we are talking about here is conceptual, not literal, and will show you how to do effective marketing, central to the evolution of any organisation. We will show you how to set up a marketing system that strengthens business, whatever country it is in, and however your people are involved, whether as a marketing student, a product, brand or marketing manager with budget responsibilities, a Director or you the CEO who wants to better empower or manage their resources, whether for themselves and / or their staff and / or your shareholders.

To spread the word or gospel, we've often thought about franchising, networking, writing a book, running seminars, all a bit tedious, partly because the target market is global and partly because the content is useful for several business lifestages - for students (to fast-track learn), for marketing managers (powerful action checklists to help them do their jobs better), and for directors / CEOs to help them **empower** more effectively - and whatever country you are in. So we are offering the marketing communication blueprint online at www.smartermarketing.co.uk for a token fee. The purpose of this book is to introduce the formula.

And it is well worth using - it's both obvious and enlightening, it's basic yet crucial, frighteningly simple and it's the best start point in putting together a profitable marketing communication system. But it's also more than that. The formula is an easy to remember expression of the critical dynamics that affect your business everyday. **It's a framework for juggling the big issues in your head. It will help you weigh up the big picture.** It's an easy way to conceptualise a strategy, or measure a proposal that's put to you. Finally, it's absolutely proven to create incremental growth, whether you're in the service, packaged goods (both low and high ticket price products), leisure, charity, financial, retail/distribution sectors, whether you are selling to businesses or selling to consumer end users.

The formula you are about to see will revolutionise your business thinking. It will help you focus on the desires of individual customers. How?

Because in an increasingly complicated business world, it will help you keep your feet on the ground as the media landscape fragments and customer choice explodes. Apply this formula to unlock your business potential.

It will show you how to generate net extra profitable sales and brand growth, using creative techniques that re-introduce the all important 'personal touch', to achieve mass awareness of appealing and relevant messages **amongst the people that really matter to your business.**

The book is written in plain simple English – for people in business who want to do proper marketing, whether these people are practising marketing managers, aspiring students or empowering directors. It's the task of CEOs to guide them.

The book gives you the action & management plan if you want to do it all yourself, the DIY model. My marketing company TBDA will do it all for you if you want the extra resource and expertise, the DFY model! As a firm of 'profit detectives' TBDA shows clients how to maximise profits from each of their end user customers by making the most of their data & crm assets, using their unique 5 Stages of Data pathway.

SMARTER MARKETING *'Be a smarter marketer, be in control'*

Stage 1

The formula that is the crucial foundation of effective marketing communication and profitable business growth

Stage 1 - **the proven business development formula**

Contents

Welcome to Stage 1

The critical task of marketing is to sell more product, generate more revenue (top line sales and bottom line profit) through creating and managing demand from the right people - in short, helping these people get what they want.

As a marketer you are playing with shareholder funds (private or public) to effect product value.

Here's how to spend your marketing budget wisely.

This is our best practice formula for increasing brand revenue, market share and accountability. It is based on years of experience in business, developed by our UK based Marketing Agency. As the media landscape continues to become increasingly fragmented and difficult, as customers take more control of the buying process, we find that this formula and its implementation procedures are massively helpful in guiding us to focus on the priorities that really build a brand's critical mass. Therefore we use these techniques in our day-to-day work designing marketing programmes and crm strategiess for our clients, both large blue-chip companies and smaller to medium sized companies. We've been doing this for over two decades and will continue to use the proven techniques in the Agency to create marketing communications that change people's behaviour and persuasively secure more loyalty from target customers.

Here it is. It's simple, memorable and easy to apply. Keep it to yourself and use it to focus and guide your efforts.

The formula that is the crucial foundation of effective marketing communication and profitable business growth is this:

ms = p x rp™

market share (sales) = penetration x repeat purchase

... where market share = your product's share of the total value & volume of its product category purchased in a given time period, say a year, in a given territory, country or region (i.e. how much of your product is purchased compared to purchase of your competitors products).

... where penetration = number of customers (end users or intermediaries) you have buying your product in relation to the total number of qualifying priority / target customers (who could buy your product) in your trading territory. It's all about maximising new customer acquisition, generating first time purchase. The crucial issue is keeping your customer proposition attractive and irresistible – creating real competitive advantage through compelling niche differentiation. Use research to check how people perceive your product, whether it fulfils their needs, how it ranks versus alternative choices. Find some people who have stopped using your product and ask them why? We will be covering this later in Stage 2.

... where repeat purchase = share of product category repertoire i.e. the number of times on average people buy the product category (of which your product is a part) in relation to the number of times they buy your product versus competitor products in a given time period, say a year. For any product category, very few people buy just one product name, one brand. They usually have a small range of favourite names, a repertoire. Brands are recruited into or rejected from the repertoire by marketing stimuli, such as ads, word of mouth, PR, direct mail, internet surfing, social media, new product launches and developments. The critical task is to maximise your product's share of a customer's repertoire. This is how you build loyalty. Additionally where relevant, you also want to increase transaction value or weight of purchase. So, **rp** includes the frequency of purchase % amount purchased & spent. It's all about maximising value & retention of known current customers. Again, we will cover this in Stage 2.

In summary, what we are saying is that market share (or sales) is a function of **p**, the number of people who can buy, and **rp**, the number of times they buy more than once in a given time period and the amount they spend. So more market share, or more sales, requires more penetration and more repeat purchase and more revenue per transaction.

For example, say you have a 5% market share at the moment and want a 10% share. Or say you don't know what your market share is but you want a 100% growth. This means you have to have twice as many people buying your product (**p**) in the same quantity as your current customers or twice as much product being bought (**rp**) by your current customers. If only life were that simple! In reality you must develop both revenue streams, because the market isn't standing still. Your competitors aren't idle and people's tastes aren't static. If your product isn't being bought, someone else's is. So you can never sit on your laurels. You constantly have to work on **p** and **rp**, to understand other product choices people have and to know whether your product is the most desirable and easily available. So for example 10% more business from current customers, 10% more new customers and 10% extra transaction value could be 33% growth... and 30, 30, 20 could be 100% growth, you do the maths for what you want.

Depending on your product type, one of the elements may be more important. For products that are not purchased frequently, like vehicles, plant, warehouse equipment or furniture, **p** is crucial in the annual marketing plan (although rp is important when replacement is due, and for recommendation). For products that are purchased frequently, like stationary, safety clothes, lab equipment, some computing equipment, maximising share of repertoire, **rp**, is also crucial.

If this seems pretty damn obvious, like motherhood, why is it so important? Here's why. It's all to do with being responsible for money (budget) which is not yours – any marketing communication budget being spent that does not pro-actively address these issues must be seriously questioned. We'll say it again – don't spend any brand budget unless the money is directly building these fundamental revenue streams of p and rp and you can measure it. Think about your budget, how is it being spent? If it is not quantifiably and measurably strengthening p or rp, review it. Can the money be better spent?

For example, is money spent on sponsorship the wisest use of the company's funds? Research has shown that after many major international sporting events, the public does not remember the name of the brands that paid a fortune to be 'lead' sponsors. Now don't sit there and try and justify it. We're not saying it should be banned. Think about it. If sponsorship is relevant and harnessed to the above 2 core issues, then fine. If it isn't, it is a flagrant waste of valuable company funds and the world is littered with corporate directors guilty of such funds misappropriation. Enough said.

This next statement is very levelling. For any organisation, business or brand, there are only two real sources of business and revenue growth:

1. **Current customers (i.e. intermediaries or end users) and the amount they spend**
2. **New customers (getting lapsed ones back or new target prospects) and the amount they spend**

The $ms = p \times rp$ formula crystallises what you must do to maximise both those sources and maximise the profit of each customer. The key to understanding your needs as a business is to understand your customers' needs first. The common element is the individual, the human being.

Remember that it is **individuals** that make purchases or influence them. They make them not just for themselves, but also for their professional needs, their image, for peer group approbation or to suit their environment. And they make them within a preferred repertoire (the choice of brands within any given product category), recruiting and rejecting brands from this repertoire depending on their experiences and outside stimuli, whether off line or on line e.g. ads, promotions, word of mouth, first experience, reviews, social media recommendation and so on. Never forget customers usually have an ever widening choice and that all the other options together are a much bigger slice of the options cake than your one brand. During a customer's journey to purchase, the opportunities to be influenced away from your product are abundant. Knowing why people buy other products than yours is critical; we cover this in Stage 2.

Remember that there are only **2 sources** of revenue and growth, current customers and non-customers. Current customers can be frequent purchasers and/or end users, or infrequent ones. Non-customers are either brand new, or lapsed.

Remember also that there are only **2 types** of purchase, first time purchase from efficient penetration of your target market... and then subsequent or repeat purchase, whether light, medium, heavy or advocate, whether loyal (mostly buying your product and occasionally others) or promiscuous (mostly buying competitive products and occasionally buying yours).

Better measuring and controlling the development of these 4 elements **will** generate growth, why, because $ms = p \: x \: rp$ - market share = target market penetration x repeat purchase. Or looking at it another way, more sales (ms) = more penetration x more repeat purchase.

As we said before, the formula is an easy to remember expression of the critical dynamics that affect your business. It's a framework for juggling the big issues in your head. It will help you weigh up the big picture. It's an easy way to conceptualise a strategy, or measure a proposal that's put to you. Also, it's a crucial way of benchmarking your business and marketing strategy (this is covered more in Stage 2).

Some business people have worry beads, some stress balls, desktop executive games or calming routines. Now you have a formula that imbues an inner calm and outwardly projects an air of confidence, because it's a real judgement and planning tool. The following table outlines a matrix of the key marketing variables that budgets and activities must affect. The ongoing aim is to test different activities and their effect on total sales. Stick with things that work well and don't allow them to be changed (such as when new staff or managers are trying to prove their presence) unless it is proven that something else works better to strengthen, or protect, total sales.

	Total market	Your product	%
Product sales (units or value)	**Xx**	**x**	**ms%**
Is it up, down, same, i.e. change on previous period	$\uparrow, \rightarrow, \downarrow$	$\uparrow, \rightarrow, \downarrow$	
Number of people buying product category	Yy	y	p%
Is it up, down, same, i.e. change on previous period	$\uparrow, \rightarrow, \downarrow$	$\uparrow, \rightarrow, \downarrow$	
Number of times bought in period	Zz	z	rp%
Is it up, down, same, i.e. change on previous period	$\uparrow, \rightarrow, \downarrow$	$\uparrow, \rightarrow, \downarrow$	

ms is a function of **p** and **rp** for your product in relation to the total market for your product category. If the market is static and your product's **p** or

rp increases, then your product's market share will increase at the expense of competitive products. Conversely if the market goes up and your products **p** or **rp** stay static, then your product's market share will decrease to the benefit of competitive products. Plus all the other variations of course. You need to think this through for your business and it might be that you choose to benchmark your product against key competitive products or a hero brand rather than the total market.

These are the key dynamics to juggle in a product's growth strategy, what you have to do to strengthen your product in relation to competitors and the total market.

This puts into perspective the true value of a marketing budget. If your budget is fixed, you probably can't outspend your competitors to build **p**. But if for example you can increase repeat purchase, **rp**, then you've done the same thing without spending more money.

Influencing your product's share of the total repertoire of products people buy in your product's category is the acid test of marketing effectiveness.

How do you do this?

We've given you the formula. This might be enough for you. Burn this into your mind – let its simplicity constantly check your efforts every working day and those of your team. Let it be a measurement mission for which every marketing communication activity and expenditure has to be ranked and justified. Constantly ask yourself – does this piece of activity maximise

ms = p x rp, which activities do this better? Don't just do the same old communications activities that have been done before. If you have any doubt about an activity's effectiveness, if you are concerned an activity has inherent wastage or cannot be properly measured in terms of effect on sales, then try something different or new, as long as you can test it first and measure its effectiveness on sales and profits. Test, measure, roll out. Test, measure, if better, roll out. But stick to the things that work, be careful of purveyors of new-fangled techniques trying to steal your mind and budgets! I call them 'magpie marketers' because they love the latest technology trinkets and waste tons of budget playing with them without being able to measure impact on profit.

As we said, this might be enough for you and you may feel sufficiently experienced to know what to do next. Now would be a convenient time to leave the book and start using the formula in your planning.

Because what you must do now is apply the formula to your business and your people (internal, e.g. departmental managers and external e.g. channel and supplier personnel), and use the formula to set your own specific marketing objectives.

For those of you wishing to carry on reading, here are some guidelines:

- Describe and quantify your target market. Who are they, why are they interested in you, how many are they and where are they?
  E.g. are your customers local or national or international – think about it, they might be national, but they're local to where they can physically get your product. Are they young, old, male or female, rich or poor, national or international? <u>Visualise them, their lifestyle, their responsibilities and influencing potential, their workplaces, their interests, the media they consume.</u>

- Describe your proposition – what is the benefit or advantage of your product and why is it special (versus competitors) – would **you** buy it? Then thinking of how you've visualised your customers above, why on earth should they be interested in buying **your** product?

E.g. does your product meet a need, does it meet an emotional need or a practical one, is it unique or a commodity (one of many doing the same thing), do you provide a good / better service? What extras and added value can you offer to make customers really warm to you, want more of you versus the alternatives?

- Describe competitor choices – what would **you** buy from all the product choices available in your product category? – put yourself in your customer's shoes:

E.g. does your product meet a need better, how do people benefit, what are its advantages? How can you keep your product proposition more appealing than your competitors' propositions?

- Understand the repertoire purchase cycle i.e. frequency of category purchase per year, 2 years, 3 years, 5 years:

E.g. when someone buys your product or one like yours, how soon is it before they buy it again and what do you do in between to keep your product in front of their mind? (This is particularly important for products where there is a long period of time before the product category is bought again). Staying front of mind in an elegant way is critical.

- Work out if there is a way of increasing transaction value, by helping people to understand the advantages to them of buying more on a single purchasing occasion. Amazon does this brilliantly, upselling, cross selling, so do a lot of adult information websites!

- Describe how people get your product? What influences your sales?

Number of sales-staff	*is it enough, is it*
Number of distributors / intermediaries	*duplicated, are there*
Number of outlets	*gaps, are there new*
The internet	*or easier ways for*
	people to get your
	product?

- Describe how you will generate demand for your product. How will you communicate persuasively with your target market without wasting money? How will you prove you haven't wasted money and demonstrate accountability? How will you influence people to keep buying your product...we will cover this in Stage 2.

- Describe how you will grow profit through building customer value and brand revenue, by doing something better and smarter than your competitors.

So now you must break down your objectives to address how you are going to get to where you want to go, both conceptually and numerically. Say we were talking to you now, but it's not now, its 1 year, or 2 years from now... what has to have happened for you to be pleased with the success... what threats addressed, what opportunities harnessed, what strengths capitalised on. Don't go mad, prioritise and focus on a few key activities that you can realistically achieve. And in a time scale in which you can achieve them.

Not bad value so far!

But what is it easy to forget or get out of perspective? Yes, the person who makes the purchase, the individual. Think about it. It's an individual that makes a purchase, whether they influence the purchase or actually buy it, or actually consume it. An individual is like you and me, a human being that has feelings, good days and bad days.

Individuals make purchases for themselves & their professional or business needs. You have to manage what we call the purchase incubation period – the amount of time, thought or research given to a purchase depends on its size, price ticket, longevity, number of purchase influencers. Obviously this has to be taken into consideration in your planning.

Individuals are either 'current' customers or 'new' customers. If they're 'current' they could be 'frequent' or 'infrequent' purchasers, loyal or promiscuous. If 'new' they could be 'lapsed' or 'target'. This is why the ms = p x rp formula is so apposite. It makes you focus on the key communication elements that create market share, sales value or profitability. The individual customer has more and more choice, they are the hunter now, not the product telling them what they want. Marketing is much more complicated now than it used to be. Our lives are more complex, there are far more pressures on our time, whether at work or in leisure. Future success will depend more on how effective marketers are in using the available information channels to influence target customers' attitudes and subsequent product purchase choice / behaviour.

That's it for Stage 1. We said earlier that the formula is a self-auditing power tool, enabling you to see the way ahead from where you are now. You now have the opportunity of moving on to Stage 2. This will show you how to manipulate penetration (**p**) and repeat purchase (**rp**) in order to strengthen market share of your product or service. Here are some introductory points.

Stage 2 – introduction: the 6 power steps to profitable success

Stage 2 is all about taking the right action – there are 6 key steps to successfully implementing the $ms = p \times rp$ formula to manage customer relationships. Following these steps will allow you to achieve the following:

- Build **p** – relevant **p** – amongst best target prospects (remember the 80 / 20 rule, the minority of customers buy the majority of your product), thereby getting more new customers interested in your proposition.

- Increase **rp** – building commitment from your current customers.

- Build your share of repertoire, getting more people to buy your product instead of your competitors. Sometimes this is called 'frequency' or 'weight' of purchase, but this is a very impersonal, esoteric phrase, (often used as sales promotion objectives), disassociated from the rationale behind people's buying behaviour.

- Better manage customer relationships through data segmentation, getting the right information on the critical buying levers for different groups of people – learn all about Perception Gap Analysis™ and FeedBak™

- Generate and measure incremental revenue and ROI, return on (marketing) investment – learn all about SalesTrak™

The price is tremendous value for the extra detail & 'how to' appendices on www.smartermarketing.co.uk. It is probably way too cheap and we'll probably put it up. But we've got to start somewhere, so you're lucky to be in early on. Nowhere else can you get for this price such a practical, proven action plan blueprint to build your market share, which is yours to keep and to keep referring to.

Our promise to you

To create net extra profitable sales and brand growth,
through one-to-one marketing that re-introduces the all important
'personal touch', to achieve mass awareness
of appealing and relevant 'buy me' messages
amongst the people that really matter to your business.

There's literally thousands and thousands of pounds worth of usable and proven techniques here…

… Proven for famous business to business brands like Fujitsu, Viking Direct, Polycom and Caterpillar

… Proven for famous retailers like Office Depot, Marks & Spencer, Co-op, Costco

… Proven for high ticket price services like Explore Worldwide Holidays, Europcar car rental, Panasonic consumer durables

… And many more not so well known names in office furniture, hotels, pubs, bakers shops, heating suppliers, rail services.

I'll share crucial data manipulation that is required to understand your customers better, not just their value, but also their perceptions and motivations, what makes them tick, what the critical buying levers are.

I'll share how to set up 'test' versus 'control' scenarios so that you measure incremental benefits in total sales revenue and brand image.

I'll share the critical amount of information you need on individual customers for successful relationship marketing – too much data and you'll get bogged down, too little and you're uninformed.

I'll share the basics of what to do with current end-user customers to maximise your product's share of the total repertoire of products they buy in your product category.

I'll share the basics of what to do to recruit new customers.

In summary, I'll show you **how to build your business around the end user customer**, to treat your customers how <u>they</u> actually want to be treated (not how <u>you</u> think they want to be treated). This is what good future marketing is all about, creating success from new, incremental, revenue development (whichever way the market is going), not just holding your own as your market changes.

Stage 2

The 6 best practice steps / tools for successfully implementing the growth formula in Stage 1

Stage 2 – the 6 power steps to profitable success

In the manual toolbox, not the book…www.smartermarketing.co.uk

Stage 2

Here are the 6 crucial steps of B2B marketing communication that will help you to better build and manage relationships with customers (influencers and buyers) and...

- BUILD MARKET SHARE (OR CREATE EXTRA PROFITABLE SALES) THROUGH STRONGER CUSTOMER COMMITMENT

- MAXIMISE FUTURE INCOME STREAM

... using 'personal touch' marketing techniques.

SOME TYPICAL ISSUES A MARKETER HAS TO ADDRESS

Although your specific objectives vary from product / service to product / service, there are some underlying requirements to address:

- Protect or strengthen market share of large / core products (strengthen USP, unique selling proposition(s))

- Grow share of smaller products (explain benefits of proposition differences)

- Cross sell new products (differentiate rationale from other products)

- Fight competitors (define competitive edge)

- Convert SWOT (strengths, weaknesses, opportunities, threats) analysis into an action plan

- Measure effect of marketing expenditure, reduce wastage, find cost savings or economies of scale

- Underpin core brand values / USP comprehension e.g. quality, world-class, trust, performance, range, whatever your key 'performance' words or phrases are

- Understand changing distribution systems (impact of new media and new distribution channels, the internet and web marketing) on customer behaviour).

WHAT ARE THE 6 STEPS?

1. How to get, analyse, interpret and understand 'hard' data on sales and 'soft' 'behavioural' data on customers. This data will help you to better diagnose the action agenda for targeted, relevant communications to different customer groups to maximise their profit contribution.

2. How to keep **current** customers and build their value, thereby engendering loyalty and maximising the profit from each customer. Use FeedBak™ to improve your contact strategy.

3. How to get **new** customers through highly targeted communication that builds awareness, desire and trial. Use 'joined up' marketing to give customers every opportunity to decide whether they want to accept your invitation to enter into a dialogue with you and be on your growing database.

4. How to tactically link 2 and 3 to enhance 'trade marketing' or local marketing and drive demand to specific geographical areas, trade channels or individual outlets, thereby supercharging budget effectiveness.

5. How to set up a detailed analysis and tracking solution for evaluation and evolution. Using SalesTrak™ to measure the effect on sales and attitudes and get a ROI (return on investment).

6. How to harness internal employee energy and get staff on board with the approach and detail i.e. getting everyone pointing their efforts in the same direction, beating the competition in satisfying customers' needs.

KEY CONSIDERATIONS

Firstly, the key to understanding your business needs is to understand your customers' needs. The common element is the individual, the human being:

Remember that it is individuals, human beings, that make purchases. They make them not just for themselves, but for their professional or business responsibilities too. And they make them within a preferred repertoire (the choice of brands within any given product category), recruiting & rejecting brands from this repertoire depending on their experiences & outside stimuli, whether off line or on line e.g. ads, promotions, word of mouth, social media interaction. Never forget customers usually have an ever widening choice and that all the other options together are a much bigger slice of the options cake than your one brand.

Remember that there are only **2 sources** of revenue and growth, current customers and non-customers. Current customers are either frequent or infrequent purchasers, non-customers are either brand new, or lapsed.

Remember that there are only **2 types** of purchase, first time purchase from efficient penetration of your target market... then subsequent or repeat purchase, whether light, medium, heavy or advocate, whether loyal (mostly buying your product and occasionally others), or promiscuous (mostly buying competitive products and occasionally buying yours).

Better influencing and measuring these 4 elements **will** generate growth. Why? Because ms = p x rp, market share = target market penetration x repeat purchase.

Secondly, understanding customer service expectations is pre-requisite to everything else in business. Never forget the difference between the 'golden rule' and the 'platinum rule' (courtesy of Tom Peters and Jay Abraham):

- The 'golden rule' is to treat customers how **you** would like to be treated, very social and polite, but no good for business.

- The 'platinum rule' is to treat customers how **they** want to be treated, not how you think they want to be treated, not how you want to treat them.

There's a huge difference between the two business attitudes. Success will increasingly come from harnessing the difference between these rules, through a better understanding, not only of peoples' needs, but also their perceptions and motivations. How do you do this? By getting data, or information, i.e. knowledge, on individual customers, from those who want to give it. Not masses of data, however, otherwise you'll be walking in treacle, because it's easy to be enthusiastic and collect too much information, which can actually hinder analysis and interpretation. Too much information is as bad too little.

Relevant customer data, or information, is the crux of being able to treat people how **they** want to be treated. By relevant, we mean only collect information that you will use, data that will better help you to influence customer behaviour – we'll address this right now and it is very important.

Step 1

Getting, analysing and understanding the right 'hard' and 'soft' behavioural data on customers, in order to help you diagnose the communications agenda better, and work towards maximising the profit of each customer.

Understanding data is the basis of understanding customers. You're probably already analysing data on your sales. This is 'hard' transactional data. If you're selling directly to end user customers and not through intermediaries, you should be doing a RFV transactional analysis to establish the recency, frequency and value of purchases by different types of customers. This will enable you to rank customers by value, from 'one purchase one product' to 'multiple purchase multiple products', and better understand patterns across different customer types or segments.

Of course you do research and analyse competitive dynamics. Plus, you can acquire, and might already have, lists of names and addresses of customers and prospects or leads.

However, it's not always easy to link these things:
- By turning data, which is passive, into information for action
- By seeing the opportunities from a customer's point of view (remember the 'platinum rule')
- By using the information to build relationships with influencers and end users, such as better targeting of relevant information, anticipating wants.

To do this you need 'soft' data, quite simply more information than just sales, on your customers. Sales happen 'after' people have made a decision. They give no indication of the thought processes 'before' purchase. Getting this information will help you understand, even predict, thought processes and therefore increase your influence on purchase decisions. The first stage is to determine **exactly** which types of individuals / businesses **actually buy** into your brands / services (and competitors).

Profiling known purchasers of your brand will tell you this. If you've already done profiling, don't be disappointed. Consider this. When did you last do it? Is it time to do it again, in more detail? For example, what about comparing new customers versus long standing ones. Is it time to compare your profile to that of key competitors? Would it help to compare your profile to that of a benchmark brand i.e. a brand image in another market that you aspire to and that you'd like your customers to see you on the same level as, in your market?

Knowing exactly **who** buys your products is essential for targeting activity better in the short term, but absolutely crucial in determining both trial and loyalty strategies for the medium and long term.

So, how do you do profiling? – use a national classification system such as SIC codes to identify type and size of business. Consult your country's DM Association. Apply the profiling to the recency, frequency, value transactional analysis of your customers, so that you can see which types of customer are most valuable to your organisation.

An alternative is 'tag' your product with a short questionnaire for a few months – see appendix 1 on www.smartermarketing.co.uk for the information you need to know so that you can start to visualise and organise your customers into understandable groups, based on their type of business location, size, usage of / relevance and attitude to your product. You may need to adapt the questions depending on your business, these are examples that need to be creatively designed to encourage response. Sometimes, it's possible to incentivise people to return the questionnaire with a prize draw, ideally for cash (cash creates the best response, we've tried all sorts of things, VIP visits, sponsor benefits and so on, cash is best).

Profiling is critical, but it's just the start. You not only need to know **who** buys what specifically, what type of company they are and where they come from... but to do proper personal touch marketing... you need to know **why** they buy...and **what else** they buy...why they **don't** buy... and what will make them buy more. And you absolutely need to discover customer **perceptions** (UBPs, unique buying / pull points) versus head office **propositions** (USPs, unique selling / push points)...from current **and** non (lapsed **and** new) customers.

How do you find all this out? You use **Perception Gap Analysis**™ research to identify, measure and quantify the perception gaps in what people actually think of you versus what you want them to think. PGA actually quantifies the differences between how people perceive you and how you'd like them to. This research technique is powerful because it's a quantitative and qualitative hybrid, providing dynamic information to understand your customers and guide your decision making process. And because it's quantitative, you can use the information to help deeper analysis, interpretation and segmentation of your customer data. It is not expensive so keep doing it, at least once a year, to refine and refine and refine... see appendix 2 on www.smartermarketing.co.uk for an overview of how to do Perception Gap Analysis™. Here's an example of why it is so important.

Company X is a very large electrical wholesaler in the UK. They provide everything form light fittings to plugs, cables, security systems and outdoor lighting, for both businesses and consumers. They have over **160,000** product lines. Another company, a publishing company, provides a regular monthly update of prices for **60,000** electrical products (drawn form Company X and its competitors) in return for a monthly subscription. Company X wanted to offer a competitive service and obviously wanted the launch to be successful. PGA research was undertaken to 4 of Company X's key customer segments:

1. Electrical contractors already getting information on the publisher's CD
2. Electrical contractors not getting the CD
3. Non-electrical contractors already getting the information on CD
4. Non-electrical contractors not getting the CD

The research had to determine the pricing policy, the creative positioning of the new service, the reasons why people would (or would not) buy the new service form Company X.

The research showed a low level of loyalty to the publisher's CD and the opportunity for a really easy estimating package to be included which would differentiate the Company X offering from the publishers. It also highlighted the need for different creative positionings for the different segments of customers based on what their critical reasons for purchase were.

The test launch beat forecasts with a significant number of customers subscribing to the new service straight away. Average sales to these customers have since increased. Follow up contact has revealed that this is due to these customers feeling that Company X is providing them with something really useful – the pricing of products and an estimating package in one hit.

Use the Profiling & PGA information to help you decide on the information fields you want in your customer database, so that as you collect names and information on them, you can build a database of known customers and segment them into groups with similar characteristics.

Use the information to build a database of your customers, but more importantly, a database of the people who influence the purchase of your product and buy it. Segment them into groups with similar characteristics. Don't expect to do the job in one period, one year. It does require a bit of an investment attitude, although the returns can be quite quick. This is not a project with a start and finish date like a promotion, web or advertising campaign, although the response mechanisms of these activities should be feeding in names of 'interested' customer leads. It is a process, an attitude to customer service, a way of treating the key people in your customers' organisations and communicating with them to build their commitment to your brand. It's a process that will be there when you've left, been promoted or whatever. It is a revenue building legacy that must be continued, developed and refined. The ultimate aim is to have and maintain a database of all the people (as they change) that buy / influence the purchase of your product so that you will be able to interact with them in a way they will like and enjoy.

This is how you increase your product's share of the repertoire of products customers buy for your product category. That is 'loyalty'. Obviously some customers will not want to interact. No problem. Always ask customers if they want advance information, thought leadership content and offers from you. Concentrate on the ones that do. Get that right and the rest will evolve.

The database and the information in it are your 'crown jewels'. This is because they are people you know either buy or are interested in your product and who have asked you to interact with them. As the channels of media communication continue to fragment, the power and cost effectiveness of being able to communicate directly with people who have requested it will grow and grow, to the extent that a customer database should become a business and balance sheet asset.

If you haven't got a customer database, start now. If you have, improve. In step 2 we will demonstrate why a customer database is a business asset. And in step 3 we will show how to invite new customers to join your database through 'joined up' marketing.

Getting a basic database going is straightforward, as are certain procedures required to keep it up to date, so get a data specialist to help you – talk to us, TBDA, or ring the DMA for guidance. The profiling and perception information will facilitate your data analysis, segmentation, data interpretation, so that you can improve your customer contact activities. Obviously it is not a one off process, although it might feel like it the first time you do it. It is a constant planning process, analysing your customer segmentation data, the consumption patterns, visualising what customers are doing.

What software should you use? To start with and if your customers are a few thousand / tens of thousand records, Access or Excel is adequate. If bigger numbers, use a SQL database. This will help you do queries and selections of the right groups of people to contact. As you get more data, for example from the activities in steps 2 and 3, you will be able to do more detailed analyses, including data mining, modelling, further refining segmentation. Here you will need more specialist help, talk to CRM specialists, again check with your local DMA or IT vendor (or the team at TBDA) – the outcome is to establish customers' preferences and behavioural propensities and the resultant profitabilities for your business. But be careful. Don't take your eye of the ball. Your task is to better serve each customer group. Don't let the IT solution and cost take over the marketing efficiency and effectiveness agenda. Only do it if it is financially profitable i.e. you get more revenue back than the extra sophisticated personalisation costs.

With the increasing number of touchpoints a customer can have with an organisation, many companies are realising the importance of creating a 'single customer view' database, an SCV – aggregating several sources of data into unified customer records i.e. so that people's names and contact details only appear once on the SCV even though they appear in more than one of the data sources. This is crucial because it means you can do queries and selections based on key behavioural criteria for targeting your campaign messages during the year.

In summary, here's a case study on how we presented the need for Recency, Frequency, Value analysis (RFV) and PGA to a Company that handles a lot of industrial materials. The RFV will show the breakdown of who the business comes from. It will therefore determine the 80/20 Pareto rule for the Company and segment the current customers. In turn, the Value part of the analysis will indicate the importance of these different segments, with implications for:

A. the amount of marketing budget to be spent on each segment to maximise that segments spend with the Company

B. the method of communication with each segment, e.g. sales rep versus telemarketing versus direct mail versus email / web.

The PGA will refine A) and B) further. By doing 32 one-to-one in-depth interviews and completing 72 full telephone interviews (based on either 4 or 8 distinct customer segments determined by the RFV analysis) we were able to discover **for each of the different customer segments:**

- Any differences in decision maker / influencer scenarios
- The reasons for the current level of business with the Company, including:
  a) competitive strengths and weaknesses of the Company's offering

b) satisfaction, or not, with product / service elements of the Company's offering

- The potential for increasing sales spend with the Company including cross sell, up sell, plus any 'missed' opportunities
- The critical purchasing triggers that would make people buy more
- Any preferred method of communication and preferred offers.

All of the above will have a huge impact on A) and B) above and will create a 'contact strategy' for each of the customer segments that will optimise the use of marketing funds, in order to maximise sales from both current, and lapsed, customers. Thanks to the PGA findings, we will also be able to follow contact strategies that have the best chance of working because we have already determined the critical purchasing levers that will generate more business, via the communication methods, and any offers, that the customers want.

In summary, this is how to understand customer needs and motivations, or rather the motivations, perceptions and needs of the key people in your customer organisations. So now you have to stay top of mind with your target customers. How are you going to do this? – we call this a 'leave behind' strategy, memory jerkers. This means you must contact key customer individuals at 'ripe' times. The following chart relates this to buyer behaviour, we call it the circle of life, as far as customer purchasing is concerned. It's fairly simplistic, but it's a start... see over...

Circle of Life / Lifestages

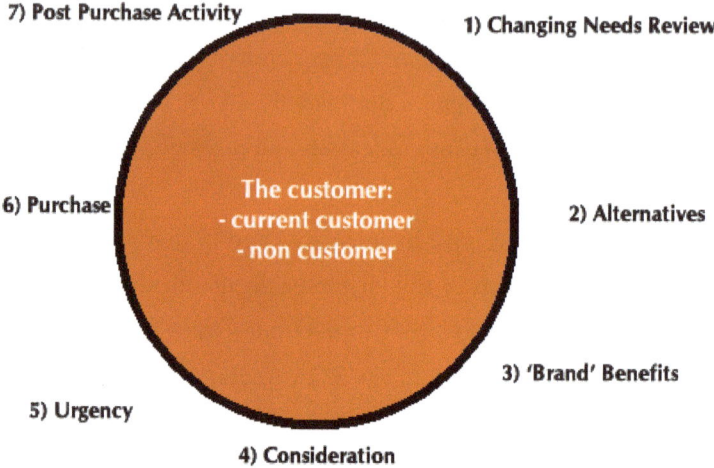

7) Post Purchase Activity

1) Changing Needs Review

6) Purchase

The customer:
- current customer
- non customer

2) Alternatives

3) 'Brand' Benefits

5) Urgency

4) Consideration

People vary the amount of consideration and research they do before buying, depending on the product type, the number of people influencing purchase, its price and the purchase frequency. It's often a case of being on the approved supplier list, which is reviewed at specific intervals. You'll need to establish these dates for each of your customers.

Your activity needs to reflect the behaviour of your key customer individuals. At some point they will review their needs, 1). They will assess the alternatives open to them, 2). This will be based on the knowledge they have on your product category, you and your competitors, or information they can get, such as from your call centre, your sales team, your website through search engines and directories, social media interaction & word of mouth. They will shortlist a range of brands and assess their respective benefits.

There will be a consideration process and a period of incubation. During this process you need to have registered your brand, its proposition and create a sense of urgency with 'an offer', 3)-5). The customer makes a decision and there's a purchase, either your product or someone else's, 6).

Post purchase activity is important, 7). If your product was bought, then you treat them like a current customer, see step 2. If your product was not bought, don't give up and run for the hills. Keeping a database of non-purchasers is valuable, because they may become purchasers in the future, if wooed correctly. A good action is to find out **why** they didn't purchase you this time – again, perception research (PGA). And the circle goes on.

So how do you get some kind of control of this circle, how do you get onto it?

Now to step 2 - keeping current customers and building their value.

If you haven't got any current customer names, go to step 3 (getting new customers) and implement it using the best targeting criteria available. Alternatively study step 2 to understand why it's important to collect names. When you've 'captured' a customer name, treat them like a current customer. It is absolutely crucial to collect names & contact details of your current customers, or people 'interested' in your product, (whether from promotions, web / digital activity, advertising and direct marketing responses), so that you can start a dialogue with the ones that want it, draw them more into your brand (versus competitors) and hopefully develop & earn loyalty. The governments and European Community are tightening up on privacy, data protection is getting stricter and the controls on direct communication methods will continue to get tighter to protect the individual customer.

Next is step 2, how to build commitment from current customers, how to start building real loyalty, using FeedBak™.

Step 2

How to build commitment from current customers; the real issues in loyalty promotion.

For **current** customers, the required action is to 'keep' them, build purchase frequency, loyalty, commitment and value, so that they buy more of **your** product than similar products in the same category; in short, maximise your product's share of repertoire and increase frequency / weight of purchase, i.e. the rp in ms = p x rp. This is what you do:

- Send* &/or stimulate (see below) relevant messages (depending on your knowledge of the business), thought leadership content (e.g. research), benefits and purchase stimuli. The relevance will depend on the knowledge of the customer types you have gained from step 1. Include some exclusivity, a reward – but don't over egg it. Test 'with' and 'without' a reward. People don't always want an offer, just (up to date) information, news or reassurance, insight content if you have it (or can commission it), or a 'thank you' (see thank you strategy below).

*test and compare mail, telemarketing, e-mail, SMS, social media (sharing thought leadership material to create leads) whatever seems appropriate for your product. How often do you communicate? On average, monthly to 3 or 4 times a year, at 'ripe' times for your product and market. Some companies offer the facility for customers to sign up for regular newsletters. Again it depends on your product or service and what you want people to do with the information. Social media has its own fast evolving protocol – find the online forums that are relevant to your product and engage; decide whether you need a Facebook, YouTube and Twitter strategy so that those people that want to can get involved (a key purpose is to find the people that want personal messages from you, so they register their email address and mobile). The power of personalised one-to-one communication is that once the benefits of your proposition are understood and liked, you're in a preferred choice situation and don't need to keep pounding home the message, like you do with advertising. Depending on your product category and its repeat purchase cycle, the cost-benefit analysis of direct or digital marketing should not necessarily be compared to just the next sale, but to the total product sales over the year or longer, or even the number of times a customer is likely to buy the category in an average year / longer period. This called 'average customer value'. The more they know about your product and its relevance to their needs, the more they'll feel better about your product and the more they'll end up buying.

- Whatever type of communication to customers you are using, whether it's mail, e-mail, web / digital or telephone, always ask questions on usage of and attitude to your product. Include a short questionnaire in order to get knowledge about the customer and their business – influencers and decision makers, likes and dislikes, reasons for purchase / non purchase of your product and competitive products – so that your database is not just a list of names and addresses, but has 'soft' information on usage and attitude. This U&A technique is called FeedBak™. From all our experience, from all the years we've been using this technique, we know there are between 10 to 15 crucial pieces of information you initially need from a customer to build a good relationship with them. Don't get loads more information, you'll flounder. Only collect information you can use to strengthen your relationship with the customer. It is this information that you use to decide what searchable fields you want to put on your database (see appendix 3 on www.smartermarketing.co.uk to see a typical list of questions, you can adapt this for your situation). If you are asking the questions online, FeedBak™ is split between levels 1-4, level 1 being the most crucial data to start a relationship. Obviously you are not going to get feedback from everyone straightaway, but what is crucial is that it will build up over several communication programmes, thereby building a valuable company asset. Some people will never give you information, it doesn't matter. Just remember the Pareto principle, you will get response from the people that are interested in having a dialogue with you, and they may be part of the 20% of people that account for 80% of your business. When creating your questionnaire, always ask yourself *"why do I need this information? Will it improve my database segmentation? How will I use it to build relationships or better service my known current customer, or send them more relevant information in the future, or treat them how they want to be treated".* If you can't answer the question easily, don't ask for the information.

If practical, incentivise people to return the questionnaire – it's in their interest, because they are giving information that is crucial to helping you give them relevant information in the future. For the incentive, offer a suitable prize draw.

- Use the FeedBak™ research information to refine segmentation of customers into groups with similar behaviour characteristics – see appendix 4 on www.smartermarketing.co.uk to see a very basic segmentation matrix; you'll get the idea.

- Leverage current advertising, design or digital marketing investment – don't reinvent creative for the sake of it. The creative treatment of your communication should be based on current brand values and brand messages. Don't reinvent the wheel, mirror current visual imagery, for example as used in advertising and brochures – create 'gestalt' (the whole is more than the sum of the parts) – this is what is meant by 'integrated' marketing.

- Develop a referral strategy – happy customers tell other people, usually several! Ask satisfied current customers to recommend your product to people they know and explain why they recommend it (in fact ask them 'who else do they know who could benefit from your services', specific name and contact details). Do some research – ask people if they would like to do this, and what they would like in return. Will they give you a testimonial, written or ideally on video? Create a system that is run on a continuous basis, because gaining new customers by word of mouth is much easier and cheaper than cold recruitment. For example, develop a carefully chosen panel of supportive 'bloggers' – these can be active customers or industry commentators, who are grateful to share privileged content you provide.

- Develop a 'thank you' strategy, this could be linked to the referral strategy. This is important because it builds up the 'feel good' factor in your customer (a financial services company sent a 'thank you' note to their current customers to mark the company's 100 year anniversary, in return they netted over £3 million worth of extra business... not bad for a bit of 'personal touch' marketing).

- Measure the **total** sales effect, not just promotional responses such as vouchers. This is called SalesTrak™, see step 5 for full details. For now, here is an abbreviation, to put into context the practical budget issues of test marketing and not scare you off. Yes, you should do all the above on a test basis first. Don't change your business practices until you feel comfortable with the processes and you've ironed out the wrinkles. SalesTrak™ procedures described more fully in step 5 are:

  - create a 'test' area and measure / compare sales for suitable time periods before, during and after the activity versus a 'control' area (see step 5)
  - do telephone research 'before' (week or more) and 'after' activity (week or more after project duration) to samples of relevant customer individuals.
  - create ROI (return on investment) model to justify roll out.

Two further thoughts:

a) The process of building commitment and loyalty from customers is as follows: the key opportunity is giving your customer the opportunity to tell you what they want, not what you think they want (through getting the right data). This in turn leads to better information and service (through FeedBak™). This in turn leads to more sales (through SalesTrak™). This means you have a dynamic interactive relationship with your customers, not a static one (with you preaching).

b) Set up a satisfaction survey system. Measuring people's satisfaction against expectation is crucial. Was the product delivered on time, was it the right spec, if there were any problems between time of order and time of delivery were you notified before you discovered the problem and were the problems dealt with professionally and to your satisfaction, would you recommend it, when would you like a follow up contact. Is there one thing that could be improved? Any negatives should be probed in a telephone call or visit. The survey can be asked after the purchase on a one to one basis. Or a questionnaire can be included with the delivery note. Feature an incentive to encourage response by return, all completed returns to be entered into a monthly / quarterly prize draw, such as some unique added value benefit such as VIP treatment at an event.

If your business is in the service sector (such as wholesaling, catering supplies, office supplies) you might want to ask about quality of service, breadth of product choice, value for money and so on.

A reference is given in the last example of appendix 3 on www.smartermarketing.co.uk .

Step 2 summary – here's an interesting chart. The shaded boxes illustrate the importance of a customer database to optimising **rp** and sales revenue. It also introduces **p**, which we will cover in the next step.

Making the *ms* = *p x rp* formula work to build demand

1. Start with the quick win, current names, the shaded boxes, this generates extra sales with targeted information and promotions by staying 'top of mind'
2. Generate new demand in 'matched' targets / catchment area(s), the white boxes
3. Where relevant, generate demand in niche markets, first shadow box
4. Generate more sales from current marketing spend – use simple response mechanic to get new names interested in 'brand', second shaded box, 'joined up' / holistic marketing

COMMUNICATION VISION

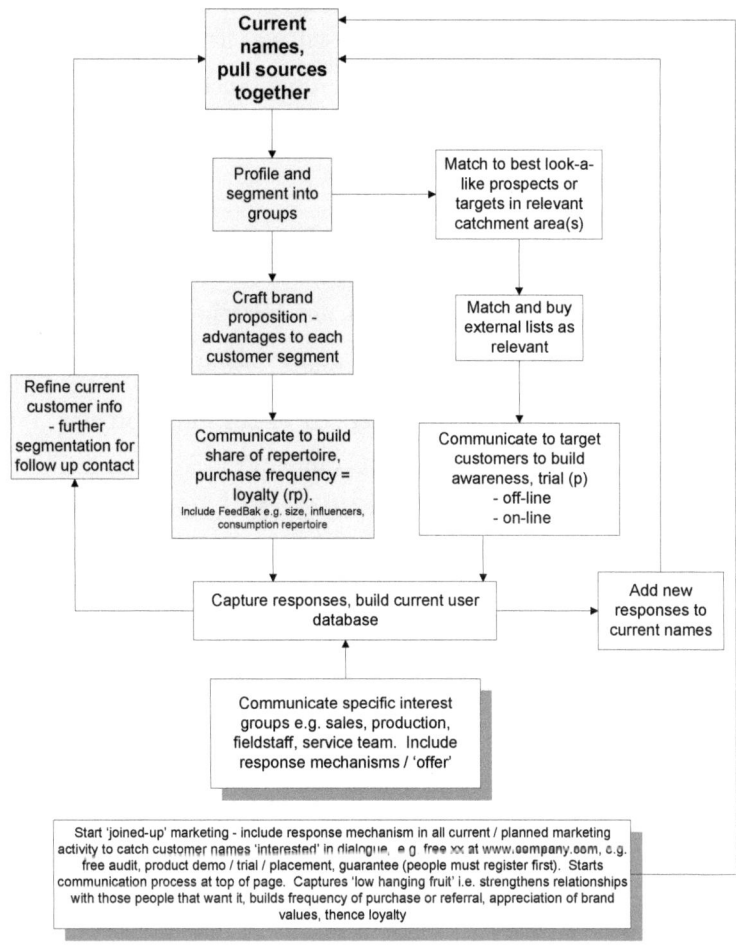

Building business equity and creating a business asset from communications expenditure

Step 3

Getting new customers

What is key is to use current customers' names to identify best potential non customers - by individual organisation and key individuals' names in each organisation.

Non customers are either 'new', potentially coming into the market, or to be courted from other brands, or 'lapsed' i.e. have stopped buying your product, or buy it very infrequently, in preference to someone else's (find out why they are lapsed using the Perception Gap Analysis research from step 1).

For non customers, the required action is to increase **penetration** by encouraging **trial** / re-trial or switch purchase i.e. at least getting your brand into their repertoire or onto the approved supplier list:

- From profiling analysis (see Stage 1) of current customer name and address information (e.g. size of company, location, industry sector), identify types of organisations with the highest potential to try your product and brand switch – this is because **new** customers are likely to be similar in profile to **current** customers, unless you have a new proposition for a new target customer.

- Send* / distribute relevant benefits & trial / switch messages. Include a purchase incentive as affordable / if necessary. Test 'with' & 'without' a reward – this is an 'invitation' to target individuals to join with your brand proposition, so you might need a stronger incentive than for current customers

*compare roles of personal contact, response advertising (on & off line), mail, telemarketing, trade magazine inserts, e-mail and internet / digital marketing, exhibitions and events. If you want to do mailing, source business lists from list brokers, talk to your local Direct Marketing Association, or ask us at TBDA. They will guide you on sources of lists for post mail and e-mail & how to negotiate rental prices based on net names used. If you want to know more about internet marketing (current customer contact strategy, search engine optimisation/PPC, promotional links programme, lead generation / traffic building techniques, optimising Linked In), again ask us at TBDA or check your local DMA.

- Do 'joined up' marketing – the biggest missed opportunity in the marketing agenda is harnessing the benefits of what we call 'joined-up' marketing. Year in, year out, marketing teams spend valuable corporate funds (the marketing budget) on different parts of the marketing mix – ads, digital, promotions, PR etc, yet there seems no system of pulling it all together. This would be achieved by simply asking people if they want to be kept informed on exclusive product, event or offer news - easy by registering their address, email or mobile phone number and adding to, or even creating, the database. So much valuable marketing budget is spent on awareness, trial, getting new customers on board, it's important to 'keep' these customers by having a dialogue with those that want it. See appendix 5 on www.smartermarketing.co.uk for a visual overview.

- Gain U&A (usage & attitude) research feedback via a simple incentivised questionnaire to get knowledge about the customer and their business – the influencers and decision makers, the reasons for purchase / non purchase / likes / dislikes – i.e. FeedBak™ (as previously described in step 2). Use this information to build your database. Think clearly what information (data) you want from new customers, so that you can give them more relevant information and better service in the future.

- Use the FeedBak™ research information to guide segmentation of customers into groups with similar behaviour characteristics. – see appendix 4 on www.smartermarketing.co.uk to see a very basic segmentation matrix.

- Leverage advertising investment as described in step 2 – don't reinvent creative unless you need to – use what's already being used. Synergy and integration is important – keep it simple

- Measure the **total** sales effect, not just promotional responses such as vouchers. This is called SalesTrak™, see step 5 for full details. For now, here is an abbreviation, to put into context the practical budget issues of test marketing and not scare you off. Yes, you should do all the above on a test basis first. Don't change your business practices until you feel comfortable with the processes and have ironed out the wrinkles. SalesTrak™ procedures described more fully in step 5 are:
  - create a 'test' area and measure / compare sales for suitable time periods versus a 'control' area (see step 5)
  - do telephone research 'before' (a week or more) and 'after' activity (a week or more after project duration) to samples of relevant customers.
  - create a ROI (return on investment) model to justify roll out.

Once you know a new customer has been acquired / re-acquired and their name is added to the database, they become a current customer and should be treated as described in step 2.

Steps 2 and 3 are contact strategies for **current** and **new** customers. It's not a project with a start and finish date, it's a process, or system, that once you've started you just keep doing to continue to strengthen your relationships with customers and subsequent revenues. This is how you build customer loyalty. Obviously budgets need to be realigned for this process, but as one senior lady marketer once said to us, "this is what I call proper marketing", i.e. not traditional broad brush stroke marketing communication which increasingly wastes a lot of valuable marketing funds, because of media fragmentation and increasingly discerning customers (many are becoming fed up, and immune to, being bombarded with either crass or untargeted 'buy me' messages and shock tactics).

Looking at the summary chart you saw at the end of step 2, **p** is represented by the white boxes.

Making the *ms = p x rp* formula work to build demand

1. Start with the quick win, current names, the shaded boxes, this generates extra sales with targeted information and promotions
2. Generate new demand in 'matched' targets / catchment area(s), the white boxes
3. Where relevant, generate demand in niche markets, first shadow box
4. Generate more sales from current marketing spend – use simple response mechanic to get new names interested in 'brand', second shaded box, 'joined up' / holistic marketing

COMMUNICATION VISION

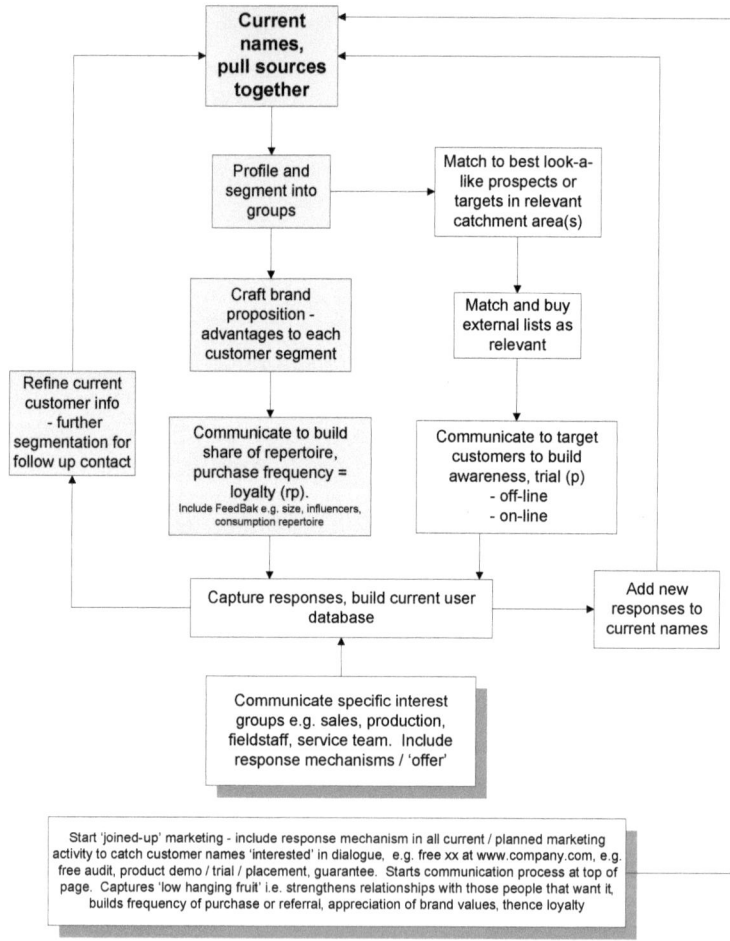

Building business equity and creating a business asset from communications expenditure

Step 4

Tactically linking steps 2 and 3 to distribution hot spots, strengthening trade marketing efficiency, getting trade customers gagging for you!

The fact is that whilst steps 2 and 3 are great missions, budgets can often compromise action reality.

This step may or may not be relevant for your business.

Step 4 – here we are going to look at tactics for driving demand in target channels, outlets or geographical areas. Firstly we'll look at end user targeting tactics. Secondly, we'll look at targeting trade customers.

a) end user targeting around key trade outlets - both steps 2 and 3 can also be used tactically, to enhance 'trade marketing' or local marketing. Where required, you can **drive end user demand to specific geographical areas, trade channels or individual outlets** in order to address trade sector weakness, national account, geographical and / or competitive threat issues, thereby supercharging budget effectiveness. Many marketers confuse the term customer between trade buyer and the end user. It's easy to fall into the trap of concentrating too much on the trade customer at the expense of generating end user demand. It's too easy to think that the priorities are all about pricing and convincing the trade about advertising commitment and that all other marketing activity is secondary. This is treadmill marketing, not very inspiring, and certainly creates a gap between what you'd like to do and what you almost feel forced to do. Here's how cleverly used direct marketing can bridge that gap...

HOW DIRECT MARKETING BRIDGES THE 'CUSTOMER' GAP TO BUILD TRADE MARKETING EFFECTIVENESS

Who is the 'Customer'?

How do you reconcile: **Trade Customer marketing**
and
End user Relationship building?

Communicate with individual end users (in the catchment areas of key trade outlet locations) to "educate" them about your brand and how / when / why to use it, to generate demand and extra sales by driving them into specific purchase destinations.

At the same time, tell Trade Customers that demand is being generated, through highly targeted promotional advertising in their catchment areas and that people are being driven to them. This will help your Sales Managers negotiate:
- Enhanced support of your products
- Listings for new products

This is the strongest way to 'Bridge the Gap'.

See case studies after the next section, b).

b) trade customer targeting – in most countries and market sectors there are a number of very large trade customers, national / key regional accounts, which are critical to a successful distribution strategy for your business. They are demanding and put constant pressure on your trading practices and margins. The advantage is that because these trade customers are few in number they can be managed on a personal one to one basis through senior sales managers.

However there are also many smaller trade customers where it is often uneconomic to manage on a personal one to one basis with your own sales staff. Thus intermediaries are used, such as wholesalers or distributors. Their business models are high volume and low margin so that the end user customer price is not too high, although usually higher than prices in the larger trade customers' outlets. They tend to carry many thousands of lines and are unable to give attention to any one line. Their focus of attention is the many smaller trade customers.

There is therefore an opportunity for the brand owner to start building relationships with these smaller trade customers using one-to-one 'personalised' direct marketing techniques, so that they order your product from their wholesalers or distributors. Again, the more you can introduce the 'personal touch' into your dealings with this large number of smaller trade customers, the more they will choose to enter into a dialogue with you and favour keeping your brand used, stocked and / or promoted in their outlet.

The process is a) identify the relevant database(s), b) rank or score the customers for your type of business, c) contact them and ask if they would like a direct dialogue with you (obviously explain the advantages), d) ask them how they want to be communicated with (e.g. post, email, phone), e) build a database of these valuable 'opt-ins', f) communicate accordingly.

The following diagram describes this procedure. We are using the UK grocery trade as an example, describing how manufacturers can build a direct dialogue with smaller trade customer outlets that buy their stock from wholesalers and distributors. There is a brief written commentary and some case studies.

The diagram represents a technique for building distribution and loyalty amongst smaller businesses, in this case independent outlets in the UK grocery trade. The first box represents the need to identify suitable databases of the target customer universe. The second box describes how to select the types of outlets you want. The third box describes how to start the communication process and segment the database according to feedback and response, and the final box indicates methods for building relationship momentum.

1) *Source* Quality Databases Of Channels
WR Knowledge Store (Independent Retail – 40-70K*)
CGA (On Trade / Foodservice – 140K*)
CGA Off-Trade – 35K* (* outlets)

2) *Segmentation* Of Channels / Outlets
Select databases
Tele-research & / or direct mail outlets & / or rank / score
Gather category data:
i.e. how much space allocated, find brand distribution points, find competitor distribution points, preferred source of supply

3) *Build* Category Specific Database
Create mechanics to drive distribution
and build database:
e.g. Newsletter / DM packs, POS, Vouchers.
Build response database

4) *Manage* / Database Management Of Channels
Ongoing data build
Ongoing analysis of data and profiling of outlets
Deliver communications plans / contact initiatives:
i.e. distinguish those outlets requiring physical sales calls, direct mail /email relationships, quarterly newsletter, and annual awareness programme

This schematic represents a proven strategic and implementation framework for how we build loyalty and revenue for clients' brands in two key channels, where it can be notoriously difficult to achieve sustained business development:

- the independent / convenience retail sector / off trade

- the on trade / foodservice sector (hospitality / leisure industry)

It is based on experience and expertise gained over the years from working with several large fmcg companies (some case studies attached).

What we have learnt is that it is crucial to be able to measure the effect on **total** sales, not just sales represented by promotional / voucher redemption. This is because people react positively to a communication and buy your product without necessarily using the promotion. From our research tracking we know that 2 to 8 times as many people actually buy without using the offer or voucher as do, due to loss, forgetfulness, 'pride', inertia and so on.

Therefore it is crucial to launch the initiative in two phases:

Phase 1 – ensure the activity is run in a 'test' area and that there is a suitable 'control' area where the rest of the business mix is the same but the 'test' activity is not run. Set up a procedure to measure total sales through the trade. We do this with SalesTrak™. The difference in sales between the 'test' and 'control' areas is down to the 'test' activity (because the rest of the business and marketing is the same across both areas). See step 5 for a fuller description of SalesTrak™.

Phase 2 – once the ROI has been verified, the programme can be rolled out as required across the country.

BEER MANUFACTURER CASE STUDY

The client required a communications strategy to be created for the UK off trade.

Initially all off trade channels were researched and a route to market created for each.

From the above segmentation strategy 32,000 independent off license businesses were identified. These we teleresearched and individual outlet data were gathered, examples of questions were:

- How many cases of beer sold per week?

- What brands of canned lager stocked?

- Where lager sourced from, e.g. Booker cash and carry etc

The answers to these questions enabled the database to be further segmented in order to create a relevant and affordable contact strategy / activity timetable. In summary this resulted in the following:

- A physical sales call file (2,000 outlets)

- A 20,000 mailing file which would receive 6 weekly mailings with money off coupons redeemable at C&C

- A list of non stockists with small potential in the category who received one mailing a year, namely a thank you Christmas Card.

On average, voucher response was 19%.

Following the above activities the database was analysed according to sales growth potential and further ranked according to promotional responsiveness.

AMBIENT YOGURT LAUNCH

The client sourced a database of UK independent grocery retail outlets. A list rental arrangement of 35K independent convenience stores and grocers was agreed - cost £8,000.

This was further segmented down to the top 7,000 by store turnover, product category range and square footage.

The client created a quarterly newsletter campaign accompanied with a personalised letter, 2 coupons (time release) and shelf talker POS.

Respondents were segmented and the newsletter was tailored accordingly.

Sales effect – established product, facings and POS.

CONFECTIONARY BRAND LAUNCH

The client sourced a database of UK independent grocery retail outlets and merged this with their own manufacturer's physical sales call file. The result was a Direct Mailing file of **30,000** outlets.

A newsletter bulletin was created (accompanied by personally addressed letter) giving category management advice, product news and coupons relating to new brand launches. The newsletter cost £0.45 per issue.

Coupon response averaged 11%, creating a specific segment of coupon responsive customers.

Sales effect – a key new product was launched and successfully established. The programme is still running and the client was also able to fine-tune their physical sales call cycle.

SOFT DRINK MANUFACTURER

The client sourced a database of UK independent grocery retail outlets and merged it with their own sales database to ensure no duplication.

They ranked and scored the outlets based upon pre determined ideal retailer profile.i.e. location near educational establishment, size of drinks chiller and presence of lottery terminal.

A sales call file was supplied to a third party sales team for a POS distribution drive.

The store profile data was used to create a segmented contact strategy based on the type of relationship the brand should have with the target outlets and the frequency of communication, e.g. those outlets requiring regular physical sales call, those worth direct mailing with regular poster & coupon campaigns and those worth less frequent mailings e.g. Christmas Seasons Greetings awareness and couponing campaign.

Sales effect – the client's new brand took substantial market share from carbonated brand leaders. The activity is now incorporated into the manufacturer's sales teams' call cycles and promotional campaign activity budgets.

BISCUIT MANUFACTURER LOYALTY PROGRAMME

A syndicate of manufacturers sourced and bought a database of **70,000** outlets (Ind Grocers, C Stores, CTN's and Forecourts).

They teleresearched the universe of outlets and shared the costs based on their questions, brands involved and the number of outlets they were individually interested in.

For the biscuit manufacturer there were several key questions, for example:

- How many feet do you allocate instore to biscuits?

- Which of the following brands do you stock?

- Where do you buy biscuits from and on what frequency?

From this activity **65%** of outlets answered the questions, which led to a profiled database of **40,000** outlets, form which a direct mailing file of **30,000** outlets was created.

The client created a quarterly newsletter bulletin accompanied by a personalised letter, questionnaire and money off coupons to be redeemed at Cash & Carry outlets. The value of the coupons varied according to the distribution level of the different biscuit brands. A **27%** response rate was achieved. Cost per issue was £0.55.

The client built a coupon response database of **8,000** outlets that was analysed regularly to identify large biscuit stockists.

Prior to Christmas a file of regular responders was created (**1,600**) and these outlets were physically called on by sales representatives.

The client ran **6** campaigns before a company merger agenda stopped expenditure.

Sales effect - from these activities total UK cash & carry sales rose by 8%, an excellent result.

Step 5

This is about evaluation and tracking, measuring the effect of your activity, in particular taking promotional analysis a critical stage further than just responses or redemptions.

Promotional responses or voucher redemptions are **not** a measure of success. They are a cost. The reality is that many customers buy as a result of the communication **without** using the offer, what we call the advertising effect. In our experience between twice and eight times as many people react positively to your highly targeted communication with them and buy **without** using the offer, so if you have a 3-5% promotion or voucher redemption, there could be up to a 24-40% positive response. Therefore measuring the **total** effect on sales, not just voucher responses, is absolutely critical to understanding the amount of incremental sales and return on investment of your personalised marketing activity.

Therefore, use the following devices:

- SalesTrak™ measures the effect on total sales. Set up a 'test' versus 'control' procedure to **measure sales throughput** generated from these specific one-to-one marketing activities. Track TOTAL sales for a couple of months before your activity starts, then during the promotional period e.g. validity of the offers, and then, crucially for a period afterwards, in order to get a reading on residual sales. The 'test' area is where you are doing targeted communications. The 'control' area is where you are doing no test activity, but where the rest of the marketing and business mix is the same. The difference between the sales data for the test area and the control area is, logically, the result of your activity. You can then compare the cost of the activity to the sales revenue and calculate a return on investment, ROI. An option to consider is to split the cost into fixed and variable costs and just use the variable cost for the ROI, because the fixed cost can be amortised when you roll out the activity after the successful test.

- Or set up a 'pre' and 'post' telemarketing survey. 'Pre' is 2 weeks before the campaign, 'post' is 4 weeks after. 'Pre' asks what products they've bought in the last month or two. 'Post' is what products have they bought in the last 4 weeks, did they get a 'communication' (mailing, leaflet, email), can they remember what it was for, what did they remember about the mailing, what is their likelihood to purchase and will this be earlier than intended. See appendix 6 on smartermarketing.co.uk for sample telemarketing questionnaires.

- FeedBak™ tracks people's usage and attitude – keep refining the segmentation from the data you get back from the questionnaires so that only relevant messages are sent to each customer group in order to build commitment to your brands. Don't worry that you only get feedback from a small percentage of people for each piece of activity. Keep including the questionnaire in all your activity. The number of people on whom you have data will grow quickly. Remember that, according to Pareto, 20% of customers do 80% of your business. Whether the percentages are correct doesn't matter. The point is that the minority of customers do the majority of your business. This helps you focus on the important ones to start with, namely the ones that give you information. Yes, there are many people who will buy your product but not want an interactive relationship with you. Never mind, the rest of the business mix will address their needs.

Finally, we come to step 6 - How to harness internal employee energy and get staff on board with the approach and detail i.e. getting everyone pointing their efforts in the same direction, beating the competition in satisfying customers' needs.

Step 6

The power of 'internal marketing'.

Now this is the exciting one. All the other steps are about interacting with customers, people outside the company. These steps represent the start of good database marketing to customers. Step 6 is the difference between database marketing and CRM. This is where you cross the Rubicon. CRM is not an IT property. It is an attitude to doing business and dealing with people. Once started it will take on its own energy and generate its own rewards. It is covered more fully in Stage 3 on www.smartermarketing.co.uk . However the crucial starting point is covered here, as the final piece in the jigsaw for ms = p x rp implementation and the management of relationships with customers.

Step 6 is all about **harnessing internal employee energy.** If you want to put the customer or consumer at the heart of the organisation (not just pay lip service to the ideal) it is absolutely critical to create a 'movement'... develop a data collection 'enthusiasm' amongst staff for customer data – feeding in names from the rest of the company, such as enquirers, complaints, call centre contacts, customer referrals, web site registrations...and of course promotional and advertising responses. It is crucial to explain to all staff, and particularly those interfacing with customers / end users, why asking for information is important. It is important because future success depends on living by the platinum rule – treating customers / end users how they want to be treated (not how you want to treat them). This can only be achieved if you collect information about them. Then the penny will drop. It must be explained to staff that information from customers is like 'gold dust' and why your customer database is your 'crown jewels' to be kept polished and up to date. We're not saying that if a member of staff is talking to a customer / end user they ask all 10 to 15 questions on FeedBak™, just some priorities (level 1) – name and email address first, then address, number of people in company, telephone number, mobile number, type of company. The other information will be gained at a later date following future contact.

Let's revisit the 'joined up' marketing visual. This is probably an effective way of explaining to staff how everything fits together and the importance of their role in acquiring vital information for managing relationships with customers / end users... (next page)...

Targeting - 'joined up' marketing (B2B)

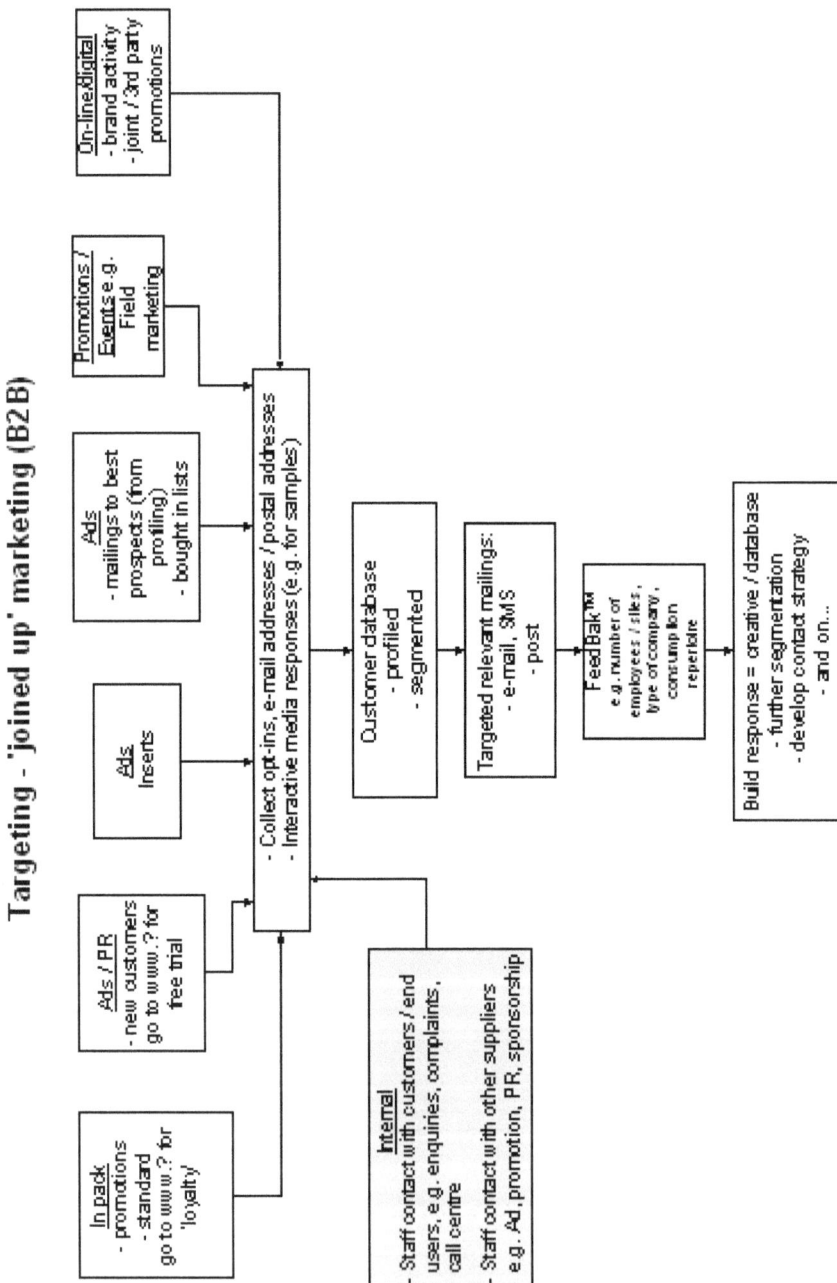

Building business equity and creating a business asset from marketing communications expenditure

So, lets review. Why is the 6-step implementation plan effective?

- It addresses & controls the critical elements of market share:

  p – getting non customers, acquisition

  rp – building commitment from current customers, retention and loyalty

- It builds a cost effective relationship-marketing model with customers that have bothered to interact, an excellent start to the whole permission / opt-in marketing bandwagon.

- It provides research information and feedback that helps you strengthen the targeting of other parts of the marketing mix, e.g. media plans, propositions, promotions, advertising, packaging – in our experience these techniques have added value to these decision issues.

- It makes marketing activity measurable and accountable

- It generates a net extra future income stream.

In one simple overview (see pages 55 & 60 for communication vision link), you can now demonstrate to staff and key suppliers how $ms = p \times rp$ works in reality and how their role is so crucial to the process and chain of activities that are critical to building the market share of the products and brand propositions they represent. In particular, explain to your Financial Director and the Board the importance of a 'database of known customers' as a business asset, and indeed an asset on the balance sheet. With increasing media fragmentation and the consequent difficulties of cost effectively getting the right messages to the right customers in a compelling manner, it is now timely to invest more resource in creatively positioning invitations to customers to 'opt in' to a dialogue with your company. This will help you to craft more relevant messages and promotions to them in the future, based on the information they give you on their organisation's profile, preferences and ordering processes. Whether you use the database and the information in it literally for building a contact strategy of personalised communications doesn't matter, the knowledge on its own, at a minimum level, is powerful for strengthening your planning and targeting. You will have crucial extra intelligence that will help influence customer behaviour.

See the next page (appendix 8 shared from www.smartermarketing.co.uk) for a one-page birds-eye overview of applying the 6-step process to improve the effectiveness of database marketing. Whether you still need convincing, or already believe in the power of a customer or member database, here is the secret of maximising its value in terms of profitable revenue generation.

Good luck. Use this 6-step process to review current performance. Create a road map of the key tasks to implement these steps that will deliver growth. Review & repeat, to keep building & refining. Train your reports to do the same. Create working parties to implement & evaluate, streamline & improve the programmes. In fact, don't let the marketing department control this process on their own, they change too often! Create a cross discipline working party to use the 6 steps as terms of reference to build the organisation around customer recruitment, retention and maximisation.

Earlier we said step 6 represented the difference between database marketing and CRM, CRM being an attitude to doing business & dealing with people. This is now covered in Stage 3 on smartermarketing.co.uk, which studies the impact marketing can have if embraced through the supply chain, through management & the financial people.

Our approach to CRM is to turn it upside down or look at it backwards. Then it becomes MRC, the management of relationships (and relevance) with customers, a business intellect, marketing and customer service attitude issue, not an IT one!

Appendix 8

THE 5Ws OF DATABASE MARKETING PLANNING

With a large database of tens / hundreds of thousand records, the secret of maximising its value in terms of profitable revenue generation is to determine the following:

WHO the most valuable customers are (repeat end-user customers versus occasional versus once only versus enquirers)

WHERE they come from

WHAT types of people / organisations they are.

WHEN they use

WHY they use (… and why they don't use more often)

- RFV (Recency, Frequency, Value) analysis will give you the low-down on the customer base – the **WHO & WHEN**, including the 80 / 20 Pareto equation for your business.

- Geographical analysis (and Profiling) will tell you **WHERE** they come from.

- Business analysis (Profiling) will tell you **WHAT** types of organisation they are.

- Perception Gap Analysis™ will tell you **WHY**.

Armed with this information, you can communicate the right message to those people it is worth communicating with (… having cleaned and enhanced the database first, of course!).

The **HOW** to communicate is then the 6 steps implementation.

The organisations that are good at doing this are at the top of their game. Think of Proctor & Gamble, Audi, Virgin, O2, Nike, Dell for example. We can all learn from them, and anyone can emulate them by adopting this strategic marketing approach.
If you know how to do this, excellent. If you want us to help, contact us on +44 (0) 1483 20 20 55, or check out Rick Pullan on Linked In.

Good luck. Please tell us about any successes or breakthroughs you achieve and whether you're happy for us to publicise them on the website, either anonymously or not.

And last but not least, how does the ordinary average business start to harness 'big data'? A recent BBC news report revealed that of **400** large companies those that had already adopted big data analytics have gained a significant lead over the rest of the corporate world. The required investment and resource cost is massive, beyond the reach of ordinary average organisations. So here's what to do... having read many white papers from leading technology companies such as Lithium, I've distilled this data explosion minefield onto one visual as a workable process... to keep building your own 'opted in' database of people... those buying, & those showing an interest... with whom you can build relationships.

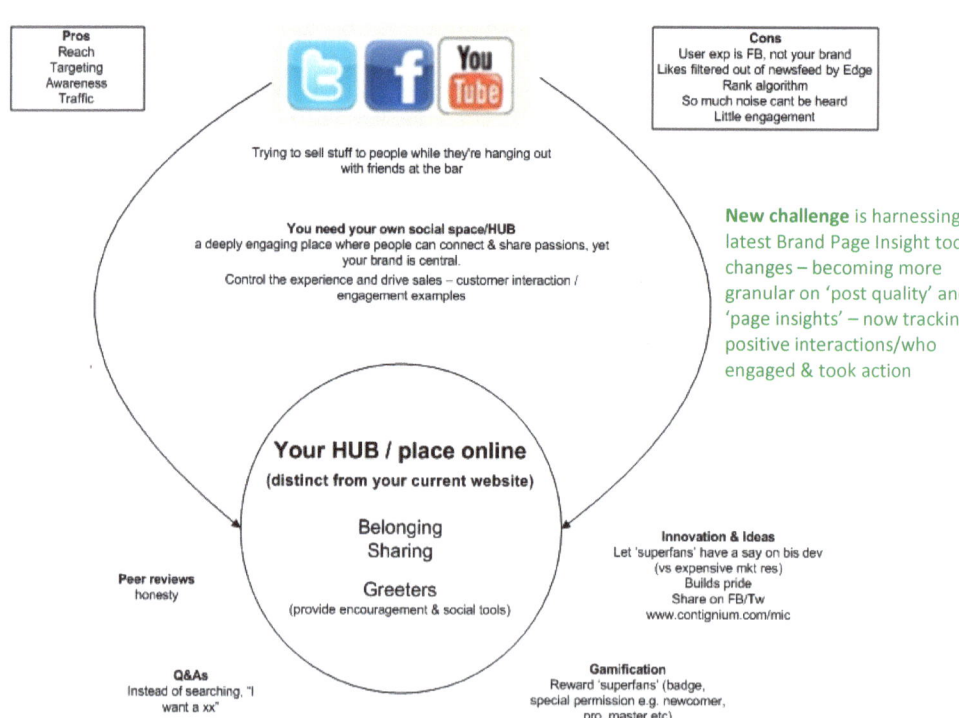

Harnessing social media to drive sales
(from more opt-ins and loyalty)

Pros
Reach
Targeting
Awareness
Traffic

Cons
User exp is FB, not your brand
Likes filtered out of newsfeed by Edge
Rank algorithm
So much noise cant be heard
Little engagement

Trying to sell stuff to people while they're hanging out with friends at the bar

You need your own social space/HUB
a deeply engaging place where people can connect & share passions, yet your brand is central.
Control the experience and drive sales – customer interaction / engagement examples

New challenge is harnessing latest Brand Page Insight tool changes – becoming more granular on 'post quality' and 'page insights' – now tracking positive interactions/who engaged & took action

Your HUB / place online
(distinct from your current website)

Belonging
Sharing

Greeters
(provide encouragement & social tools)

Peer reviews
honesty

Innovation & Ideas
Let 'superfans' have a say on bis dev
(vs expensive mkt res)
Builds pride
Share on FB/Tw
www.contignium.com/mic

Q&As
Instead of searching, "I want a xx"

Gamification
Reward 'superfans' (badge, special permission e.g. newcomer, pro, master etc)

© 2013 tbda
01483 20 20 55

When cybercrime crushes commercial trust of www.internet.com as we know it, companies without dynamic customer databases will wither, because they won't be able to talk to customers easily or cost effectively. I urge you to build and nurture your opted in databases.

So, we have gone full circle from the beginning of the book... whatever happens in the world, in commerce you need to be able to talk to your customers & prospects in your way. Use SmarterMarketing (ms = p x rp) to build your data skills – to get your current customers to buy more frequently and spend more (rp), and to get new customers (p). Here's some interesting numbers for you – if 10% of current customers buy again in the year, if 10% of them spend more with you, if you increase the number of customers by 10%, then your turnover or market share increase could be around 30+%.

Do the maths – what would 8, 12, 15% for each mean to your business – setting some KPIs would be a meaningful target for value added effort from your team. Be a bit more ambitious and the numbers really start to get exciting... 30 / 30 / 30 could give you 100+% growth.

Visualise this scenario – many CEOs are working on their businesses for an exit strategy. Here's a simple scenario, but it makes the point. The investor has done much due diligence and is down to 2 companies to buy. Both CEOs & management teams are brillant, products are excellent & order books look good. Pretty much all the boxes are ticked for both organisations. There's a final question from the investor to both CEOs... "tell me why I should prefer to buy your company". One CEO says "I have a bang up to date database with all supporting crm for all my current customers, plus people who have expressed an interest in our company... with all the right information on their preferences so that we can give them what they want, when & how they want". This CEO refers them to the balance sheet explanatory note under 'assets', that the CFO is putting a value on the database as an intangible 'marketing asset'. The other CEO deosn't say that, maybe talks about industry awards, grants to the community, visiting professorships to Harvard or something.

Which company do you think the investor would prefer to buy?

Rick Pullan - Who am I?

See me on Linked in. Graduating with an honours degree in Economics & Business Studies at Sheffield University, England, I started work with Mars as a salesman, was hauled into head office as a graduate trainee. I learnt brand management at Beecham (now Glaxo). I learnt mis-marketing at Pedro Domecq, because my bosses were ex P&Gers who thought they could bully the drinks industry with aggressive grocery marketing tactics. Mentored by Phil Luckett, John Hayter and Leonard Lavin, I grew to Marketing Director for Alberto VO5 (now a Unilever brand) in the UK when I was 28, then to MD in the Far East when I was 30, running 5 countries through national distributors where I saved the principal company from bankruptcy.

Back to the UK I became a freelance entrepreneur, then bought equity in an agency I liked before selling out to Colin Lloyd. I launched TBDA, ww.tbda.co.uk, The Business Development Agency (now True Business Data Activation) in the mid 90s with data genius Richard Organ, ex CACI, when Colin sold out to Euro RSCG, now Havas Media.

The summary is I have an uncanny 360 degree vision of commerce, the importance of 'customer experience' and the delivery of customer satisfaction.

SmarterMarketing is one of my gifts back to industry, because since I left the prescient values of ROTA at Mars, where Marketers were the Gods of cash flow creation, and revered as such, and since I learnt so much from the draconian 'loss of yield' fine on Marketing from Beecham Accountants, I have become increasingly appalled at 'marketing's' track record in Boardroom contribution. Mainly a result of poor accountability. Not trusted by CFOs or respected by shareholders. What a shower we Marketers can be! This is not just my jaundiced opinion, there are loads of media reports articulating the lament.

Hopefully this book, its formula and introduction to the fuller blueprint *(www.smartermarketing.co.uk)* manual & toolbox helps. Or I'll refund you the small cost, if you dare request it!

A special thank you to all my family, friends and business colleagues who've encouraged me to distil the ups and downs of 40 years business experience into this SmarterMarketing success system. And to the inspirations from reading, seeing or hearing Jay Abraham, Claude Hopkins, Theodore Levitt, Tony Robbins, Tom Peters, Lou Gerstner, Lee Iacocca, Richard Branson, Professor Robert Shaw, David White and the Dan Kennedy crew.

Testimonials …

"When I ran Farah Clothing Company, I used these guys as a marketing agency supplier. The results were impressive. The secrets of their success are here now. Whether you're a CEO or a marketing practitioner, ignore them at your peril. If you're a marketing student or just starting out in a marketing career, you've just hit the jackpot!"

Eric Thornton, CEO www.justteeshirts.co.uk

"Having read this stuff, I've now incorporated it into my modus operandi, use it to keep a handle on my marketing people and their suppliers, and hired the Agency to work for me! Great stuff. Well done. Tremendous value, loads of common sense and real practical ideas to implement."

Roger Hollis, former CEO, Roomservice by Cort (a Berkshire Hathaway Company) www.roomservicebycort.com

"Marketers have been accused of being expensive, slippery and unaccountable. I like the common sense practical approach here of implementing good, targeted marketing communications and measuring the effectiveness on sales and revenue of marketing spend. SmarterMarketing is an easy to grasp process to focus the marketer's mind in today's maelstrom of message clutter and increasing customer empowerment".

"Using the martial arts analogy, this is the red, yellow, green level before the brown and black of my own Marketing Payback textbook!"

Professor Robert Shaw, www.vbmf.com, author of Marketing Payback, creator of the 'Imagine, Predict, Demonstrate' infinity formula for our DMA Return on Ideas thought leadership innovation with CIMA and CIM – better results from Finance and Marketing working together

"I wish I'd had this when I started out in marketing. It's full of practical tips and checklists, the appendices are really useful. I like the way it focuses on the real marketing issues that generate profitable revenue gorwth, for any size of organisation".

Catherine Blackburn, Marketing Director, UK Drinks Company, co-creator of Red Bull success in UK, now CEO of BlackburnGarden Business Solutions www.blackburngarden.com

"The value built into this program doesn't even bare thinking about! I've worked for several large organisation all with one thing in common.... they're paying literally thousands of £££'s in the search for a marketing strategy that will help them achieve sustainable growth. It's amazing to think that you can have what all the major players are in search of for just a tiny fraction of the cost. This really is a must have for anyone in business that wants to be successful in their marketing effort and more importantly those who wish to reproduce that marketing success over and over again!..."

Mike Connelly www.smartnumber.co.uk The SwitchboardFree Call Management People

"This is the simplest, most down to earth, practical way of planning your marketing campaigns I have ever seen. Great formula and strategy for growing your business.

Mark Storrar, Entrepreneur"

""I've known Rick for over 30 years. He may not be as famous as some of the global business gurus, but he has one of the finest marketing brains I've known. There's more marketing know how in his little finger than many of the supposed marketing experts I've met in my career. If he says this is how to be a smarter marketer, go for it. I've read it all and I believe him".

RIP - Dennis Miller, CEO, UK Distributor of International Drinks brands